Original title:
Wild Whispers

Copyright © 2024 Creative Arts Management OÜ
All rights reserved.

Author: Levi Montgomery
ISBN HARDBACK: 978-9916-90-542-5
ISBN PAPERBACK: 978-9916-90-543-2

Symphony of Solitary Wanderers

In the shadows where echoes hum,
Footsteps linger, hearts succumb.
Each path a tale of dreams unspun,
A silent dance, two lives as one.

Stars above in velvet night,
Guide the lost with silver light.
Solitude, a trusted friend,
With whispers soft that never end.

The Untamed Song of Solace

In rustling leaves, a melody,
Untamed notes of wild decree.
Nature sings with fervent might,
In every dawn, a new delight.

Mountains rise to greet the sun,
In harmony, their song begun.
The river flows, a gentle sound,
In solitude, lost souls are found.

Beneath the Sky's Gentle Embrace

Clouds drift softly, dreams in flight,
A canvas painted, pure delight.
Beneath the vast and azure dome,
Hearts find peace, the soul feels home.

Winds whisper secrets through the trees,
Carrying hopes upon the breeze.
The sun dips low, a golden hue,
In twilight's glow, the world anew.

Whispers of the Fern-blanketed Floor

Among the ferns, a secret lies,
In nature's arms, the heart complies.
Soft footsteps tread on mossy ground,
In silence, wisdom can be found.

Light filters through the leafy green,
As time stands still, a tranquil scene.
Each breath a part of earth's own lore,
In whispered grace, we seek for more.

Murmurs Beneath the Canopy

In shadows deep, the breezes sigh,
Leaves rustle softly, whispers fly.
Beneath the boughs, tales softly spun,
Nature's secrets, shared by none.

A gentle hush, the forest breathes,
Life hidden well beneath the leaves.
Echoes of dreams in twilight's glow,
Where silent thoughts begin to flow.

Secrets of the Untamed Ground

Roots entwined in earth's embrace,
Silent stories, time cannot erase.
Every stone, a relic of yore,
Guarding whispers from days before.

In tangled grass, the shadows play,
Lost adventures from far away.
Footfalls soft on ancient trails,
Carried by winds, the lore prevails.

Whispers Among the Thorns

Amidst the brambles, secrets lie,
Soft murmurs rise, a gentle sigh.
Petals closed, yet hearts still yearn,
For morning light, in shadows, churn.

Beneath the thorns, a tender bloom,
Against the odds, it finds its room.
In silent strength, the beauty thrives,
Among the thorns, true love survives.

Voices of the Unfenced Heart

In open fields, where dreams take flight,
Voices call beneath the starlit night.
Free from confines, the spirit roams,
Finding solace, in distant homes.

The beat of life, a wild song,
Where every soul feels they belong.
Unfenced paths, where passions spark,
Guided by light, igniting the dark.

Tales from the Roots Below

In the dark where whispers dwell,
Tales unfold, a silent swell.
Roots entwined in secrets deep,
Nature's lore, forever keep.

Crimson leaves in autumn's dance,
Stir the earth with fleeting glance.
Buried dreams in soil abide,
Echoing where shadows hide.

Ancient trunks with stories old,
Guard the treasures, brave and bold.
Life awakens, seasons turn,
From the roots, the world will learn.

Whispered Wishes Beneath the Stars

Underneath the velvet night,
Stars like candles, soft and bright.
Wishes float on cosmic breeze,
A symphony of hearts at ease.

Moonlight bathes the world in dreams,
Woven tales in silver beams.
Each twinkle holds a secret song,
A reminder we belong.

In the quiet, spirits soar,
With every wish, we seek for more.
Boundless skies and endless grace,
In this moment, find our place.

Enigmatic Echoes of the Great Outdoors

Mountains rise with stoic pride,
Whispers call from every side.
Rivers weave through valleys wide,
Nature's heart cannot abide.

Sunlit paths and shadowy trails,
Conceal myths where wonder prevails.
Animal tracks, an ancient code,
In every step, a journey flowed.

Winds carry tales of yore,
Through the leaves, they gently score.
The wild sings its timeless tune,
A melody beneath the moon.

The Breath of Untamed Horizons

Across the plains where eagles fly,
Endless skies and dreams to try.
Whispers of the wild unfold,
Stories of the brave and bold.

Mountains touch the azure sea,
Horizons call, they beckon free.
The heartbeat of the earth resounds,
In every breath, adventure found.

Fields of gold and forests green,
In nature's arms, we seek the unseen.
The journey stretches, vast and wide,
With every step, the world our guide.

Breath of the Untamed Breeze

In the wild where whispers play,
The breeze dances through the trees.
It carries tales of night and day,
A gentle song, a playful tease.

Across the fields, it weaves so free,
Unraveled dreams on paper boats.
It hums a tune of mystery,
As nature sings with joyful notes.

Through mountain peaks and valleys deep,
Awakening the silent night.
It stirs the spirit from its sleep,
With every gust, it takes to flight.

The untamed air, this fleeting kiss,
Reminds us of the wild inside.
In every swirl, a taste of bliss,
The breeze, our ever-changing guide.

The Softest Shriek of Freedom

Across the dawn, a call is heard,
A voice that breaks the morning calm.
In every word, a lively bird,
Its melody, a soothing balm.

The world erupts in vibrant hues,
As sunlight spills on fields anew.
This softest shriek, a spirit's muse,
A promise to pursue what's true.

From shackles forged in iron chains,
To open skies, where eagles soar.
It echoes ever, through the plains,
The softest shriek, forever more.

With every pulse of life it brings,
A heartbeat wrapped in boundless grace.
It dances joy where freedom sings,
A timeless song, our warm embrace.

Lullabies from the Untrodden Path

In shadows deep, where dreams do weave,
A gentle hush brings stories near.
The night with kindness starts to cleave,
And whispers soft for hearts to hear.

Beneath the stars, the journey calls,
With every step, a truth revealed.
In nature's arms, the silence falls,
A lullaby, the soul is healed.

The path unknown, a secret thread,
Where fears dissolve like misty air.
With every note, old worries shed,
And lullabies become a prayer.

In every rustle, every sigh,
The untrodden path sings sweet and low.
For in the quiet, dreams can fly,
And hearts can heal where wildflowers grow.

Secrets Carried by the Wind

The zephyr breathes through ancient oaks,
It carries whispers, soft and light.
In every twist, a tale invokes,
The secrets lost to day and night.

From mountains high to valleys wide,
The wind unveils what time forgets.
In sighs and shivers, it confides,
In every breeze, a story sets.

Through bustling towns and quiet glades,
It spins the yarns of those long past.
With swirls of dust, in gentle fades,
The echoes linger, unsurpassed.

So take a moment, close your eyes,
And listen close to what is spun.
For in the wind, a truth that flies,
A treasure chest, where all begun.

Conversations with the Moonlit Glade

In whispers soft, the shadows play,
Beneath the stars, we weave our way.
The night air sings a tender tune,
Guided by light from the watchful moon.

The leaves rustle with secret sighs,
As dreams drift slowly through the skies.
Footsteps echo on the forest floor,
Inviting spirits to linger more.

Each flicker hints of tales untold,
In silver glow, the worlds unfold.
We find our peace in nature's hand,
In the glade where enchantments stand.

So let us share this tranquil night,
With twilight's kiss, oh pure delight.
Within the glade, our hearts align,
Conversations whispered, so divine.

Nature's Veiled Confessions

In shadowed glades where secrets dwell,
Nature whispers, casting her spell.
Ink-stained clouds conceal the truth,
In every breeze, there lies our youth.

The rivers hum with ancient lore,
As trees stand tall, their spirits soar.
Nature cradles each gentle sigh,
In veils of mist, our dreams will fly.

A flower's blush, a fleeting glance,
Reminds us of a silent dance.
Each breeze that stirs the emerald leaves,
Holds confessions the heart believes.

If we listen, the earth will speak,
Tales of wonder, strong yet weak.
In nature's arms, we find our place,
With every confession, our souls embrace.

Enigmas of the Fragrant Meadow

In meadows bright, where blossoms roam,
Each petal whispers tales of home.
The scent of earth, it lingers sweet,
Inviting wanderers, a soft retreat.

Beneath the sun, the shadows play,
With curious minds that drift away.
In every rustle, a story waits,
Enigmas bright behind nature's gates.

A symphony of colors blend,
Where time and space begin to bend.
Amidst the flowers, secrets sigh,
In fragrant whispers, dreams may fly.

So let us wander, hand in hand,
Through fragrant fields, a promised land.
Each step we take, at nature's pace,
Unraveling mysteries in this place.

Chasing the Gentle Gales

On gentle wings, the breezes glide,
Through open fields, our hearts abide.
We chase the whispers, soft and clear,
In every gust, we shed our fear.

The world around, in motion too,
With stories rich, both old and new.
We feel the dance of air so light,
As dreams ignite in endless flight.

Each whisper carries hopes and dreams,
As laughter flows in silver streams.
With open arms, we greet the night,
Embracing shadows, merging bright.

So let us run where the wind may lead,
In gentle gales, our spirits freed.
Together bound in nature's play,
Chasing the song of every day.

The Sound of Forgotten Echoes

In shadows deep, whispers arise,
From ancient tales where silence lies.
Memories drift like leaves in the breeze,
Echoes linger among the trees.

A chorus fades in twilight's glow,
The past returns in a gentle flow.
A sigh of fate in a distant night,
Lost voices dance in the fading light.

Beneath the stars, a haunting sound,
Stories of hope where dreams are found.
In every pause, a heartbeat remains,
The sound of life in forgotten chains.

As dawn awakens, the echoes cease,
Yet in our hearts, they find their peace.
A melody soft, both sweet and low,
The sound of echoes, forever aglow.

Notes from the Spirit of the Wild

In the heart of dusk, a silhouette leaps,
Nature whispers as the stillness sleeps.
Mighty trees bend to the winds that call,
In their embrace, we find our thrall.

The river flows with tales untold,
Where secrets linger and dreams unfold.
A rustling leaf, a creature's sigh,
In every sound, the wild draws nigh.

Moonlight dances on feathered wings,
The night unveils the magic it brings.
With every note from the wild's own heart,
We hear the music, a sacred art.

Together we roam, nature's kin,
In the spirit of wild, our souls begin.
So let the rhythms of the earth be found,
In every corner of this sacred ground.

Fluttering Secrets

In gardens bright, where shadows play,
Whispers linger throughout the day.
Butterflies dance on a gentle breeze,
Fluttering secrets among the leaves.

Petals unfold with delicate grace,
Each bloom a story, a soft embrace.
Hidden wonders in colors bold,
Fluttering dreams in the springtime gold.

A glimmering light in the morning dew,
The world awakens, fresh and new.
With every flutter, a tale takes flight,
Secrets shared in the dawn's first light.

The echoes of nature softly call,
In every whisper, we hear it all.
Fluttering secrets, both near and far,
A tapestry woven by nature's star.

Echoes of Untamed Souls

In wilderness deep, where spirits roam,
Untamed souls forge their ancient home.
A howl in the night, a fierce delight,
Echoes awaken the dreams in flight.

Through jagged mountains, a heartbeat thrums,
Rhythms of life where the wild wind hums.
In shadows cast by the towering pines,
We find the echoes, where freedom shines.

With eyes that glimmer, reflecting the sky,
Untamed souls soar, unbound, they fly.
In every rustle, a story we share,
Echoes of lives lived without a care.

In the pulse of the earth, we hear the call,
Every whisper, a reminder to all.
Echoes of untamed, forever they flow,
In the depths of our hearts, they continue to grow.

The Dance of Elusive Whispers

In shadows where the soft winds sigh,
Ghostly figures weave and fly.
With every twirl, a secret shared,
In a world that's never bared.

The moonlight casts a silver glow,
As echoes of the night winds flow.
A ballet of the untold dreams,
In silence where the magic gleams.

Their laughter fades upon the dew,
In the dark, they shimmer through.
A dance that only few can see,
In whispers bound to set them free.

So let your heart take to the night,
And join the waltz of hidden light.
For in this realm of veils and grace,
You'll find your own enchanted place.

Serenade of the Shy Creatures

In thickets deep, they softly tread,
Where fears and dreams are gently spread.
With flickering eyes and timid heart,
They sing a song, a work of art.

The rustling leaves, a hush descends,
As twilight's glow their journey bends.
Each note they play, a secret wish,
In nature's hand, their souls they dish.

With each shy glance, they share their hope,
In fragile bonds, they learn to cope.
Their voices blend in sweet refrain,
In every chord, a hint of pain.

So when you hear the nightingale,
Remember tales the soft winds tell.
Of creatures shy, yet full of grace,
In their serenade, find your place.

Secrets Carried by the Evening Wind

The breeze whispers, secrets unfold,
Stories of the brave and bold.
From mountains high to valleys low,
The evening tales begin to flow.

Each rustling leaf, a voice of time,
Sharing memories in soft rhyme.
With every gust, a past revealed,
The heart's emotions gently healed.

Through ancient trees, the breezes glide,
Carrying dreams, with none to hide.
In every breath, a wish takes flight,
Guided by the fading light.

Listen closely, close your eyes,
Feel the magic, let it rise.
For in the wind, the world expands,
Carrying love in gentle hands.

Murmuring Streams and Starlit Skies

Beneath the stars, the waters gleam,
A whispering, soft, like a dream.
Where silver threads of moonlight dance,
In nature's arms, a stolen chance.

The stream hums low, a lullaby,
As crickets join, a gentle sigh.
With every ripple, life unfolds,
In whispers shared and stories told.

The skies above, a canvas bright,
With twinkling gems, a breathtaking sight.
Where cosmos meet the earthly flow,
In harmony, a timeless show.

So find your peace beside the stream,
Embrace the night, let your heart beam.
In murmurs soft and starlit glow,
Feel the magic of the ebb and flow.

Roaming Shadows and Silent Calls

In twilight's glow, shadows creep,
They dance in whispers, secrets deep.
An echo of the night's embrace,
Where silence holds a hidden place.

Moonlight weaves a silver thread,
As dreams unfold in gentle tread.
Footfalls soft on ancient ground,
In these moments, peace is found.

The night is rich with untold tales,
Of wandering hearts and midnight trails.
Each shadow speaks in murmured tones,
In the stillness, the wild roams.

Through dense thickets and starlit skies,
Silent calls inspire our sighs.
We roam as ghosts, both brave and free,
In every shadow, a memory.

Whispers Beneath the Canopy

Beneath the leaves, the secrets flow,
Soft murmurs where the wildflowers grow.
Nature's breath, a gentle sigh,
In the stillness, spirits fly.

Sunlight dapples the forest floor,
As whispers weave through every door.
Life in motion, a silent song,
Where the heart feels it belongs.

The branches sway with ancient grace,
In the embrace of this sacred space.
Voices linger in the air,
In every rustle, love laid bare.

Under stars that softly gleam,
The night unfolds like a waking dream.
In this realm of soft and sweet,
Whispers echo, a heart's retreat.

Symphonies of the Untamed Soul

In wildest places, true hearts sing,
Nature's pulse is awakening.
A symphony of earth and sky,
Where the spirits learn to fly.

Every leaf plays a tune of peace,
Ebbing worries, they find release.
The rivers hum their soothing lore,
As mountains stand and bravely soar.

With every step, the heart aligns,
With rhythms sung in ancient signs.
The wild wind plays a soaring flute,
In the dance of life's deep-rooted loot.

Each creature adds to nature's song,
In the choir, where all belong.
An untamed spirit, bold and free,
In symphonies that speak to me.

Serendipity in the Wilderness

In every corner, an unplanned find,
The wild reveals what's intertwined.
A twist of fate, a path unknown,
In nature's arms, we've truly grown.

In rustling leaves, life speaks anew,
Moments rare in morning's dew.
With serendipity as our guide,
We wander forth, hearts open wide.

A glimpse of beauty, a fleeting glance,
In the wilderness, we take our chance.
In every step, the joy unfolds,
As nature's magic subtly holds.

With every breath, a chance to see,
The world's vast gifts waiting to be.
In serendipity's gentle thrall,
We find our place, we find it all.

The Sighs of Untold Stories

In shadows deep where secrets dwell,
The echoes of the past do swell.
Every sigh, a tale concealed,
In whispers soft, the truth revealed.

Lost moments dance on silent air,
Each heartbeat speaks of dreams laid bare.
With every breath, a story flows,
In quiet corners, longing grows.

Beneath the moon's soft silver glow,
The hidden paths of time we know.
Each shadow holds a starlit theme,
In every sigh, a vibrant dream.

So listen close, and heed the light,
For every tale waits for the night.
Untold stories in hearts abide,
In gentle truths, our souls confide.

The Leafy Secrets of Past Lives

In emerald crowns where whispers hide,
The stories of the ancients glide.
Each leaf, a page in nature's tome,
A rustling voice that bids us home.

Roots entwined in earth's embrace,
Shadows linger in this sacred space.
Each branch extends to lost tomorrows,
Cradling joy and veiled sorrows.

The wind carries the tales they weave,
Of lives once lived, of dreams achieved.
In every gust, the past arrives,
Unveiling truths of verdant lives.

So wander where the leaves do dance,
In every rustle, take your chance.
For hidden secrets softly lay,
In leafy whispers of yesterday.

Whispers in the Gloaming

As daylight fades and shadows blend,
The gloaming draws a gentle hand.
In twilight's hush, the secrets sigh,
As stars awaken in the sky.

Soft murmurs float on evening's breeze,
Telling tales among the trees.
The world transforms in dusky light,
As whispers dance throughout the night.

Each flicker of a firefly,
A moment passed, a fleeting sigh.
In solitude, the heart reflects,
On dreams unseen and deep respects.

So linger long in twilight's grace,
Find solace in its warm embrace.
For in these whispers lies the key,
To life's great truths, wild and free.

Subtle Echoes of Nature's Heartbeat

In quiet glades where moments sleep,
The earth breathes slow, its secrets keep.
With every pulse, a gentle hum,
The heartbeat of the wild becomes.

Each brook that flows, a song sincere,
Reflects the love that lingers near.
Among the leaves, a symphony,
Of nature's grace and harmony.

The mountains stand with steadfast pride,
While oceans whisper, swell, and glide.
In every crag, or rolling hill,
The echoes call, and hearts they fill.

So walk the path where wild things roam,
Feel nature's pulse lead you back home.
In subtle echoes, life reveals,
The sacred truth that every heart feels.

Shadows in the Tall Grass

In the whispering breeze, shadows breeze,
Dancing softly, a nature's tease.
Beneath the sun's warm, golden glance,
The tall grass sways in a silent dance.

Murmurs of earth, secrets untold,
In every blade, a story unfolds.
Glimmers of light, a magical show,
Where shadows roam and whispers flow.

Creatures hide, in the emerald sea,
Watching the world, so wild, so free.
Nature's artwork, each hue and shade,
In the tall grass, memories made.

Evening descends, a peaceful sigh,
Stars emerge in a velvet sky.
Shadows linger where dreams embrace,
In the tall grass, we find our place.

Rustling Dreams in the Meadow

In the meadow where wildflowers sway,
Dreams are rustling at the end of the day.
Colors burst in a vibrant dance,
Nature's canvas, a sweet romance.

Gentle breezes carry soft sighs,
Fluttering wings beneath the skies.
Whispers of hope linger on high,
As dreams awaken and softly fly.

Crickets sing as the dusk unfolds,
Mysteries woven, secrets told.
In every heartbeat, the meadow glows,
Where rustling dreams find a place to grow.

Beneath the stars, in lavender hue,
The night invites the heart to renew.
In this meadow of solace and peace,
Rustling dreams shall never cease.

Nature's Quiet Confessions

In the stillness, nature confides,
In rustling leaves, where silence resides.
Whispers of trees, ancient and wise,
Secret confessions beneath the skies.

The brook murmurs tales of old,
Memories wrapped in water's fold.
In the quiet, truth finds its voice,
Among the shadows, we can rejoice.

Moonlight kisses the night so fair,
A tranquil moment, beyond compare.
Stars listen close to the stories shared,
In nature's heart, we know we are cared.

Every sigh of the breeze reveals,
The hidden truths that nature feels.
In quiet confessions, our souls connect,
Embracing the peace that we all expect.

Hidden Songs of the Wilderness

In the wild, where silence sings,
Hidden songs on nature's wings.
Rustling leaves, a gentle hum,
Calling forth the wild things to come.

Mountains echo with ancient lore,
Whispers carried from shore to shore.
Each heartbeat resonates with grace,
In the wilderness, we find our space.

Streams babble soft, serene and low,
Carrying tales where wildflowers grow.
A symphony of life in every breath,
In hidden songs, we conquer death.

As twilight paints the sky with fire,
Nature's chorus lifts us higher.
In the wilderness, we hear the call,
Hidden songs embracing us all.

Tales of Forgotten Trails

In the woods where shadows creep,
Echoes of secrets softly keep.
Footsteps linger on the way,
Whispers of the past at play.

Old stones gather mossy pride,
Beneath the trees, the spirits hide.
Paths twist under canopies,
Carrying tales on the breeze.

Moonlight glimmers on the ground,
Lost stories waiting to be found.
Nature's voice, a soft refrain,
Guiding hearts through joy and pain.

In the heart of silent night,
Dreams wander without fright.
Each trail a story, deeply sown,
In these woods, we are not alone.

The Language of Lost Spirits

Here the stars speak in hushed tones,
Whispers of souls, lost to stones.
In twilight's embrace, they reside,
Echoes of lives where love abides.

Clouds weave tales, a spectral dance,
Gift of the night, a fleeting chance.
Hearts entwined in a soft sigh,
As shadows pass and moments fly.

Memory's fragrance fills the air,
Each ghostly presence, a quiet prayer.
In silence, forgotten dreams rise,
Beneath the watchful, silver skies.

Listen close to the ancient winds,
Where the past and present blends.
The language of spirits speaks clear,
In every sigh, they linger near.

Soft Songs of the Hidden Vale

In valleys deep, where soft winds play,
Melodies flow through night and day.
Nature hums with gentle grace,
In every leaf, a warm embrace.

The brook babbles a tender tune,
Under the watch of the pale moon.
Songs of the dawn, sweetly spun,
Whisper of peace, a world begun.

Where flowers bloom with colors bright,
They sing to the stars, a pure delight.
Hidden paths where wonders grow,
Soft songs echo, low and slow.

Listen close to this sacred space,
Feel the heartbeat of nature's pace.
In the vale, a heart can mend,
With every note, the soul ascends.

Breath of the Unseen World

Between the folds of time and space,
Lies a realm, a hidden place.
Where shadows breathe and silence sings,
And every moment, magic brings.

Mist weaves softly through the trees,
In quiet whispers, it does tease.
The unseen world breathes in the night,
Where dreams are born and take flight.

Each heartbeat aligns with the stars,
Eternity's glow through cosmic bars.
Life dances lightly on the breeze,
In a world that bends with gentle ease.

Dive into depths of this embrace,
Find the light in the darkest space.
In every breath, unseen, unfurled,
Lies the beauty of the unseen world.

Timeless Secrets of the Underbrush

Whispers of the leaves at play,
Hidden worlds where shadows stay.
Quiet tales from roots below,
In the dark, their secrets grow.

Crickets chirp a lulling tune,
Underneath the watching moon.
Life unfolds in subtle ways,
Unseen magic in the haze.

Beneath the ferns, the stories weave,
Life and death in webs they leave.
Nature's voice, a soft caress,
Hiding truths, both large and less.

In the thicket, wisdom blooms,
Engulfed in nature's sweet perfumes.
Time stands still, yet moves so fast,
In the underbrush, shadows cast.

Murmured Mysteries of the Twilight

As the sun begins to fade,
Softly falls the evening shade.
Colors blend, a canvas sighs,
While the day bids sweet goodbyes.

Night creeps forth with gentle grace,
Stars awaken, take their place.
Every glow tells tales anew,
In the quiet, whispers grew.

Moths flutter by, a dance in flight,
Secrets shared by fading light.
The world transforms in muted tones,
Breathing life into ancient bones.

Softly hums the evening breeze,
Carrying the song of trees.
Murmurs rise, a twilight tune,
Calling out beneath the moon.

The Grasses Sing at Night

Underneath the starlit sky,
Grasses sway, a lullaby.
Softly rustling, roots in dance,
Nature's song, a sweet romance.

Each blade whispers dreams untold,
Of sunlight wrapped in nighttime's hold.
With every swish, with every sound,
Secrets of the earth abound.

The chorus of the night unfolds,
In the dark, their story holds.
Crickets join in rhythmic cheer,
Celebrating all that's dear.

Harmony of nature's breath,
Life and love entwined in death.
The grasses sing, a night so bright,
Echoing through the soft moonlight.

Veiled Conversations in the Thicket

In the thicket, secrets spin,
Voices rise and quietly thin.
Hidden paths where shadows glance,
Moments lost in nature's dance.

Foxes wander, watchful gaze,
A silent pact through misty haze.
Every step, a whispered theme,
Veiled truths drift within a dream.

Branches crackle, stories shared,
Life's rich tapestry prepared.
In the stillness, hearts align,
Nature's bond, a sacred sign.

Conversations lost, yet known,
In the thicket, life has grown.
Veiled in shadows, bright with light,
Whispers linger through the night.

Echoes of Untamed Secrets

In shadows deep where whispers play,
Old secrets linger, fade away.
The night conceals what hearts have known,
In every glance, the truth is shown.

Fractured dreams and ancient cries,
Reverberate beneath the skies.
Each sigh a tale of love and loss,
Through moonlit paths, we count the cost.

The echoes dance in misty air,
A tapestry of hidden care.
Beneath the stars, our fears confess,
In silence, we unearth the rest.

So tread with caution, seeker bold,
For untamed secrets dare unfold.
Listen closely, hear the sound,
Of whispers lost but ever found.

Murmurs from the Untrodden Path

In twilight's grip, the wild things sigh,
With whispered thoughts that drift and fly.
Each step a choice, each choice a chance,
To waltz with fate in life's short dance.

The trees bear witness, ancient and wise,
They tell of love beneath the skies.
Their rustling leaves share stories spun,
Of battles lost and victories won.

With every turn, a new dream wakes,
In grassy fields where solitude stakes.
Through gentle winds, these murmurs weave,
A trail of hope for those who believe.

So journey forth with heart unbound,
In untrodden paths, true peace is found.
Embrace the whispers of the night,
And let your spirit take to flight.

Secrets of the Uncharted Forest

Amidst the boughs where secrets lie,
The ancient woods breathe a soft sigh.
With roots that twist in hidden ways,
They guard the past through countless days.

Crimson leaves spill tales of yore,
Of lovers lost and myths of lore.
The moonlight drips like honey sweet,
On dreams entwined where shadows meet.

With every step, the whispers grow,
Stories carved in bark below.
Through tangled paths, the heart will roam,
Finding in the wild its home.

So delve into this timeless space,
Where nature keeps its warm embrace.
Unlock the secrets, set them free,
In the forest's heart, you'll find the key.

The Lure of the Unfamiliar Breeze

A soft caress from lands unknown,
The breeze carries whispers, overgrown.
It plays with leaves and stirs the air,
Inviting dreams with tender care.

With every gust, it tells a tale,
Of distant shores and ships that sail.
It murmurs secrets lost in time,
In rhythms sweet, in silent rhyme.

This lure awakens hearts confined,
To follow paths that fate designed.
In every breath, adventure bold,
The call of life, a story told.

So chase the winds, embrace the call,
In unfamiliar breezes, find your all.
Let go of doubt, let silence cease,
And in the freedom, discover peace.

Beneath the Canopy's Veil

Leaves whisper secrets, soft and low,
Dancing shadows in the twilight glow.
Branches cradle dreams in their embrace,
Nature's breath, a gentle, fleeting grace.

Winds weave stories, ancient and wise,
Golden sunlight filters through the skies.
A symphony of life, serene and bright,
Beneath the canopy, the world's delight.

Roots entwined with tales of old,
Mossy carpets where stories unfold.
In this haven, time slows its pace,
Nature's arms, a warm, tender space.

Beneath the boughs, we find our peace,
In every rustle, worries cease.
With each heartbeat, a bond we form,
Under the trees, we weather the storm.

The Hushed Murmur of Foliage

In the quiet woods, a soft sigh stirs,
Foliage rustles, nature's gentle purrs.
Each leaf a whisper, secrets to share,
In emerald shadows, we linger and dare.

Beneath the boughs, a cool embrace flows,
In dappled light, the soft magic grows.
The air alive with a timeless refrain,
The lush green world, both calm and arcane.

Steps fall softly on the forest floor,
Echoing tales of those who've come before.
Shared glances drown in the vivid array,
As time slips softly, guiding our way.

With every breath, we sink into bliss,
A sacred solace in nature's kiss.
The murmuring leaves, a balm for the soul,
In this haven, we finally feel whole.

Beneath the Howling Moon

By silver light, the shadows creep,
Under the moon's watch, night secrets keep.
Wolves sing lullabies to the starry sky,
In the mystical glow, our dreams can fly.

Branches sway with a ghostly grace,
Echoes linger in this haunted space.
The moon, a guardian, fierce and bright,
Guiding lost souls through the velvet night.

Fog rolls in, a shroud of whispers,
Every glance holds mysteries, it glisters.
Beneath the howling moon's fierce gaze,
We find our way through the twilight haze.

A spell is cast on the restless heart,
In this night realm, shadows play their part.
With every moonbeam, dreams intertwine,
Beneath the howling moon, fate aligns.

Enchanted Echoes of the Forgotten

In forgotten realms where old trees stand,
Echoes of laughter weave through the land.
Whispers of yore on the soft winds sigh,
In shadows of time, lost moments lie.

Each worn path holds a tale untold,
Of dreams and promises, wonders bold.
A breeze carries notes of forgotten grace,
As nature cradles every heart's trace.

Misty dawns reveal secrets anew,
In silken webs where dewdrops strew.
Echoes linger, soft as a prayer,
In enchanted realms, we're lost in the air.

Remembered dances in twilight's embrace,
Fleeting glimpses of an ancient place.
In the stillness, we find our song,
Enchanted echoes, where we belong.

Lullabies of the Untamed Heart

In shadows deep, the wild things sing,
A whisper soft, as night takes wing.
The moonlight dances on secrets bare,
Hearts unbound, in their tender care.

Stars twinkle bright, like eyes that see,
The dreams we hold, wild and free.
Nature croons in gentle lull,
Softly rocking the restless soul.

Echoes of laughter fill the air,
With every note, a soothing prayer.
Let the heart wander, let it roam,
In the wild's embrace, we find our home.

As dawn breaks slow, the shadows flee,
We carry forth this melody.
The untamed heart, it beats anew,
In lullabies, both fierce and true.

The Flutter of Unspoken Dreams

In quiet corners of the mind,
Whispers flutter, hope entwined.
Each thought a bird, a gentle flight,
Chasing the dawn, embracing light.

In colors bright, our wishes soar,
Beyond the waves, to distant shores.
A tapestry of all we seek,
In silence loud, our hearts do speak.

Beneath the stars, they twist and twirl,
Dreams unfurl in a secret whirl.
With every heartbeat, they take form,
A silent dance in the night so warm.

In shadows cast, they softly glow,
A promise made in the ebb and flow.
The fluttering sighs of what could be,
In unspoken dreams, we find our key.

Visions from the Overgrown Path

Step softly now, on nature's way,
Where tangled roots in silence sway.
A wayward breeze stirs tales long lost,
In every leaf, the past embossed.

The wildflowers bloom, in colors vast,
A brush with time, a whisper cast.
Each footfall brings a story near,
In the overgrown, we persevere.

From shadows thick, to sunlight's kiss,
We wander forth, in search of bliss.
With every breath, the visions rise,
An ancient song beneath the skies.

Treasured moments hide in light,
Awakening dreams that take to flight.
With nature's pulse, our spirits blend,
On the overgrown path, journeys mend.

Resonance of the Silent Woods

In the stillness, a low hum grows,
The pulse of life, where nature flows.
Whispers carry on the breeze,
In silent woods, the heart finds ease.

Beneath the canopies, shadows play,
Time drifts by in a soft ballet.
The rustle of leaves, a soft refrain,
In every breath, the woods explain.

Echoes linger, stories unfold,
In the tapestry of green and gold.
Each heartbeat syncs with the earth's own song,
In the silent woods, where we belong.

A sanctuary, steadfast and grand,
With nature's wisdom, hand in hand.
The resonance calls, a sweet embrace,
In silent woods, we find our place.

Timid Calls in the Starlit Night

Whispers of night in gentle air,
Stars glimmer softly, secrets to share.
A trembling heart beneath the sky,
Yearning for dreams as time drifts by.

Moonlight dances on shadows cast,
Fleeting moments, forever vast.
In silence, the world finds its peace,
While timid calls invite release.

Dialogue of Nature's Secrets

In rustling leaves, a story told,
Of ancient trees and whispers bold.
Mountains hum with a thundering voice,
While rivers sing, a fluid choice.

Breezes carry the tales of time,
Echoing softly, nature's rhyme.
In every breath, a bond so deep,
Where secrets lie and secrets seep.

Soft Songs from Hidden Valleys

In valleys where the shadows play,
Soft songs rise with the breaking day.
Gentle echoes of the past,
Embracing hearts, forever vast.

Beneath the boughs, the world feels light,
Nature's chorus, a pure delight.
With each note that lingers long,
Life unfolds in a vibrant song.

The Silent Call of Overgrown Paths

Overgrown paths weave stories untold,
In silence they beckon, brave and bold.
With every step, the wild unfolds,
Whispers of journeys and adventures old.

Vines embrace the history shared,
Memories linger, gentle and bared.
Where shadows dance and secrets abide,
The silent call of nature's guide.

The Secrets That Shadows Keep

In twilight's gentle, fading light,
Shadows dance, cloaked in night.
Whispers swirl on the breeze,
Tales held tight in secret trees.

Hidden truths beneath the veil,
In the silence, softest wail.
Echoes linger, lost in time,
The unknown wrapped in rhyme.

Silent watchers, patient stay,
Guardians of the dusk and day.
Beneath the cloak of twilight deep,
Are the secrets that shadows keep.

Twinkling stars their stories weave,
Even shadows dare believe.
In their stillness, wisdom's flow,
In the dark, the truths we sow.

Nature's Unspoken Bond

Whispers rustle through the leaves,
In sacred woods, the spirit breathes.
A gentle stream sings with glee,
Nature cradles you and me.

Mountains stand, giants of grace,
Embracing skies, a warm embrace.
Flowers bloom in vibrant hues,
Painting dreams for us to choose.

In every breeze, a soft caress,
In quiet moments, we confess.
Shared secrets by the shore,
Nature holds us, evermore.

In the twilight's amber glow,
Life's rhythm lulls us slow.
A bond unspoken, deep and wide,
In nature's heart, we abide.

Hushed Legends of the Open Fields

In fields where wildflowers bloom,
Legends echo; shadows loom.
Gently swaying in the breeze,
Secrets told by rustling trees.

Once upon a time they say,
The winds could hear the earth's ballet.
Stories carried far and wide,
Of adventure, hope, and pride.

Dancing grains of golden wheat,
Capture moments bittersweet.
The whispers of the passing time,
Enchanted tales in nature's rhyme.

When twilight falls, the stars align,
Sharing stories, yours and mine.
In the fields where silence weaves,
Hushed legends of what nature believes.

Threads of Reverie in Wilderness

In the wild, where dreams take flight,
Threads of reverie spin in light.
Through the glades, a path unmarked,
In every heartbeat, hope is sparked.

Mossy stones and quiet streams,
Weaving softly through our dreams.
Footsteps echo, nature's song,
In the vastness, we belong.

Stars above, a guiding hand,
Leading us through untamed land.
Each whisper, every rustling leaf,
Breathes a story, brings belief.

In wilderness, our souls refine,
Threads of reverie intertwine.
With every step, we learn to see,
The beauty in wild, wild free.

Tales from the Untamed Realm

In shadows deep, the wild ones roam,
Where ancient trees weave tales of home.
With whispers low, the night unfolds,
The secrets of the forest's bold.

Beneath the stars, the creatures dance,
In moonlight's glow, they take their chance.
From roaring rivers to silent glades,
The stories of the wild cascade.

In haunting calls, the echoes ring,
The heart of nature starts to sing.
With every rustle, every sound,
Adventure waits, new worlds abound.

So listen close, let spirits guide,
The tales await, in dreams they bide.
For in this realm, untamed and free,
Lies the heart of mystery.

Whispers of the Forest Spirits

In twilight's hush, the spirits sigh,
Their voices dance with the breezy sigh.
Among the boughs, they weave a song,
Of ancient woods where they belong.

With every step on the mossy ground,
The echoes of time can be found.
A fluttering leaf, a fleeting glance,
Invites the curious to join their dance.

Through tangled roots and branches wide,
The energies of the forest hide.
In laughter soft, and shadows deep,
The secrets of the wild they keep.

So wander far, let magic flow,
Where nature's whispers softly grow.
The spirits call, their tales unfold,
In the heart of the woods, behold.

The Language of Rustling Leaves

The leaves converse in whispers light,
With every breeze, they take their flight.
From oak to pine, the messages flow,
In a symphony only they know.

A gentle rustle, a soft caress,
Each sound a story, each pause a guess.
Secrets shared in the pale moon's glow,
The forest speaks, if you only slow.

Through seasons change, they sing their lore,
In golden hues, or the chill of yore.
Listen closely, let silence lead,
In every murmur, a wondrous seed.

The language flows beneath our feet,
As nature's heart begins to beat.
In rustling leaves, the world takes breath,
A testament to life and death.

Ghosts Beneath the Star-kissed Sky

When stars alight on the velvet hue,
The ghosts emerge, both old and new.
With whispered tales of love and woe,
They weave a tapestry, soft and slow.

Through the night, their shadows glide,
In memories of those who've died.
In every flicker, a story told,
Of lives once lived, of hearts so bold.

So gaze above at the twilight sphere,
And in the silence, try to hear.
The echoes of a world long past,
Where dreams and shadows seem to last.

In the star-kissed night, they find their peace,
A reminder that love will never cease.
Beneath the sky, where wonders lie,
The ghosts of time still softly sigh.

Confessions of an Unfettered Spirit

I roam the fields, where dreams reside,
Barefoot in freedom, with nothing to hide.
Each gust of wind, a gentle call,
Whispering secrets, awaiting my thrall.

Beneath the sky, my heart takes flight,
Chasing the stars, embracing the night.
No chains can hold this daring soul,
In the vast expanse, I feel so whole.

Sunrise spills gold on the morning dew,
Awakening hopes, so fresh and new.
With every step, I shed my fears,
Laughing and dancing through the years.

In solitude's embrace, I find my peace,
An unfettered spirit that will never cease.
To wander and wonder, eternally roam,
In the heart of the wild, I find my home.

The Unseen Dance of Nature

In the forest's hush, a secret spread,
Where shadows whisper, and light is shed.
Roots intertwine, in a silent waltz,
Nature's rhythm, a dance that enthralls.

Leaves flutter gently, a soft ballet,
Kissed by the breeze in a playful sway.
Streams laugh and twirl, a melodic stream,
Nature's own song, a vibrant dream.

Mountains stand tall, guardians of time,
Echoes of wild, a timeless chime.
In the petals' twirl, the colors blend,
A masterpiece wrought, where sorrows mend.

In twilight's glow, the dusk does sing,
A lullaby sweet that the night will bring.
As stars join in, the dance unfolds,
A tale of nature, eternally told.

Elusive Melodies in the Green

Soft notes arise from the heart of trees,
Whispers of magic carried by the breeze.
In the tapestry of leaves, a symphony,
Elusive melodies, setting hearts free.

Birds exchange songs, a playful duet,
Nature's chorus, a sweet vignette.
The rustle of grass, a gentle refrain,
Echoes of joy in the playful rain.

In the stillness, find the unseen sound,
Each rustling moment, life's joys abound.
Every creature sings, in their own way,
Elusive melodies of night and day.

As daylight fades, and shadows creep,
The night takes stage, where secrets seep.
In this green haven, hear the call,
Melodies of nature, enchanting us all.

The Solitude of Leafy Whispers

In the quiet grove, where secrets lie,
Leaves tell stories as the soft winds sigh.
An ancient hush, time slows to a crawl,
In leafy whispers, I hear nature's call.

Branches dance lightly, embracing the sky,
Cradled in silence, the world drifting by.
In shadows of green, I find my retreat,
Comfort in solitude, so pure and sweet.

Every flutter, and rustle, a tale retold,
In the arms of the trees, I feel consoled.
Listening intently, where spirits converge,
In the tranquil moments, my soul starts to surge.

For within these whispers, a truth does bloom,
In the solitude found, there's no room for gloom.
In nature's embrace, all worries cease,
Finding my solace, my heart at peace.

Soundscapes of the Hidden Woods

In the shade where silence breathes,
Leaves whisper secrets to the breeze.
Gentle rustles weave through trees,
Nature sings with subtle ease.

Streams chuckle over rocks so worn,
Birds call softly at the morn.
Footsteps muffled on the floor,
Echoes dance from door to door.

Sunlight dapples through the green,
Wildflowers bloom, a vibrant scene.
Every sound, a story told,
The woods cradle dreams of old.

As twilight drapes its velvet gown,
Crickets play their evening crown.
In this realm, stillness reigns,
Lost in music, free from chains.

Whispers from the Burrowed Depths

Beneath the earth, the whispers flow,
Tales of shadows, soft and low.
Roots entwine with silent grace,
Life hidden in this sacred space.

The heartbeat of the ancient stone,
Echoes carried, felt alone.
Muffled footsteps, secrets blend,
In the dark, where shadows send.

In caverns deep, the old stones sigh,
Stalactites hanging from the sky.
Whispers of time, they softly teach,
Lessons found just out of reach.

In twilight's glow, they come alive,
The stories that the darkness thrives.
With each breath, the calm descends,
Whispers linger, never ends.

Celestial Murmurs of the Earth

Underneath the starry dome,
The earth hums, a cosmic home.
Melodies in the night air flutter,
A symphony of soft, sweet utter.

Mountains cradle whispers low,
Time weaves tales where rivers flow.
Moonlight kisses fields so wide,
Every shadow knows the tide.

In the hush of dawn's embrace,
Nature finds its sacred place.
A tapestry of sounds unfolds,
As the sun its warmth beholds.

Through valleys deep, the breezes rise,
With every sigh, a world complies.
Celestial songs of life abound,
In each note, the earth resounds.

Enigmatic Breezes of Dusk

As the sun dips below the line,
Breezes carry scents divine.
Whispers swirl in twilight's grasp,
Enigmas held, waiting to clasp.

Crickets serenade the night,
Stars awaken, shining bright.
The air is heavy with a spell,
Where every secret dreams to dwell.

Leaves rustle with a gentle sigh,
As day gives way to night's soft cry.
In the fading light, shadows blend,
On the path where wanderers wend.

Mysteries float on evening's breath,
Hints of life beyond mere death.
In this hour, magic weaves,
Breezes whisper, as twilight leaves.

Conversations with the Ancient Trees

In whispers soft, they speak with grace,
Their leaves like hands, in sunlight's embrace.
Each ring a tale of time so vast,
Rooted in moments, both present and past.

They listen close to winds that weave,
The secrets held, the stories we leave.
From every storm, their spirits grow,
In shadows deep, their wisdom flows.

Bark worn and gnarled, yet strong they stand,
Guardians steadfast of this land.
In silent dialogue, we find our way,
Through ancient eyes, night turns to day.

So let us pause beneath their shade,
In their presence, be unafraid.
For in their hearts, the world unfolds,
A tapestry rich in green and gold.

The Soft Sigh of Distant Mountains

In the stillness, mountains rise,
Glimmering 'neath the fading skies.
With each breath, a gentle sigh,
Whispers of ages drifting high.

The peaks hold secrets, old and wise,
Veiled in mist, where silence lies.
A canvas painted soft and bold,
Stories of nature, forever told.

Beneath the stars, they touch the night,
Cloaked in shadows, bathed in light.
Their rugged bounds, a call to roam,
In their embrace, we find our home.

Listen close, let your heart entwine,
With every echo, a sacred line.
For the mountains sigh, a hymn to hear,
In their soft presence, we draw near.

Elves and Fairies Beneath the Boughs

In twilight's glow, they dance and play,
Elves and fairies in a world of fray.
With laughter light, they weave their dreams,
Among the roots and silver streams.

Beneath the boughs, in shadows deep,
Where secrets linger and willows weep.
They whisper spells, both sweet and sly,
As fireflies blink in the dusky sky.

With gossamer wings and hearts so free,
They spin the tales of what could be.
In every petal, a song remains,
A harmony sweet as springtime rains.

So venture forth, let your spirit soar,
In the realm where magic is never poor.
For in the glen, where old trees bend,
Elves and fairies embrace, my friend.

Whimsical Tides of the Unfamiliar

The waves crash soft on shores unknown,
Curling secrets in the foam they've sown.
Each tide a tale from lands afar,
Whimsical dances beneath the star.

In moonlit nights, dreams come alive,
As whispers rise, like gulls they dive.
A melody borne on ocean's breath,
A symphony played from life to death.

With every ebb, a story fades,
But in the flow, new hope cascades.
The tides, they tease, with laughter free,
Inviting souls to wander the sea.

So touch the water, feel the call,
For in the unknown, we learn to fall.
With each new wave, let thy heart drift,
In whimsical tides, let your spirit lift.

The Lonely Call of the Nightingale

In the hush of evening's grace,
A nightingale begins to sing,
Her melody a soft embrace,
Echoing through the trees, a wing.

Silhouettes in silver light,
Whispers carried by the air,
She weaves a tale of lost delight,
In shadows deep, her song lays bare.

With every note, the stars draw near,
To listen to her heartfelt plea,
In lonely realms, she casts her fear,
A symphony of yearning, free.

Beneath the moon's watchful eye,
The nightingale keeps vigil still,
A serenade that cannot die,
In every heart, her echoes thrill.

Secrets of the Wandering Breeze

Through the fields where silence sweeps,
The wandering breeze begins to roam,
Carrying whispers that it keeps,
From valleys wide to mountain home.

It dances lightly past the trees,
Untangling thoughts from tangled roots,
A gentle touch, a teasing tease,
In playful curves, it finds its routes.

The secrets of the earth it knows,
A tapestry of stories spun,
In every breath, a memory flows,
Beneath the sky, beneath the sun.

So listen close when night descends,
To tales the wandering breeze imparts,
For in its flight, the truth transcends,
A symphony of all our hearts.

Twilight Muses in the Thicket

In twilight's hush where shadows blend,
Muses gather, soft and bright,
In thickets deep, they weave and mend,
The threads of dreams in fading light.

A brush of wings, a fleeting glance,
Whispers trail in the dying day,
They beckon souls to join the dance,
In twilight's glow, they softly sway.

With every breath, an urge to soar,
Through tangled paths where wonders lie,
The heart ignites, forevermore,
As muses call to the evening sky.

Embrace their charm, let fears dissolve,
In thicket's warmth, find peace anew,
For in their realm, we all evolve,
Creating worlds with every view.

The Covenant of Hidden Dreams

In silent realms where secrets dwell,
A covenant is softly made,
To share the dreams we cannot tell,
In whispered tones that never fade.

Beneath the stars, our hopes take flight,
In shadows cast by moonlit streams,
We weave together through the night,
United in our hidden dreams.

Each heart a canvas, blank and wide,
With colors bold that long for light,
In every stroke, the fears subside,
As visions dance in pure delight.

So hold this pact with gentle care,
For dreams are tender, sweet as cream,
Together we will bravely share,
The sacred art of every dream.

The Hushed Echo of Ferns

In the shade where ferns do sway,
Whispers of the night hold sway.
Secrets lie in dampened ground,
Nature's voice, a tender sound.

Moonlight drips on leaves so green,
In the silence, dreams are seen.
Every shadow tells a tale,
In this realm where quiet prevails.

Softly rustles every breeze,
Carrying the scents of trees.
Footsteps lost in twilight's breath,
A serene dance with quiet death.

Nature's lullaby unfolds,
Ancient stories softly told.
In the heart of ferns we find,
Echoes of the earth entwined.

Dreaming in the Ancient Woods

Beneath the arching canopies,
Dreams are woven with the trees.
Mossy carpets cradle feet,
Nature's pulse, a steady beat.

Sunlight filters through the leaves,
Weaving magic, the heart believes.
In the hush, the spirit roams,
In these woods, we find our homes.

Every rustle, every sigh,
Tales of ages drifting by.
Ancient roots that twist and turn,
In their wisdom, we shall learn.

Hidden paths and secrets shared,
In the stillness, souls are bared.
Dreaming deep in shadows cast,
In the woods, time seems to last.

The Enchantment of Swaying Willows

Willows dance along the shore,
Swaying gently, tales galore.
Whispers carried on the stream,
In their grace, we find our dream.

Beneath their boughs, we take a seat,
Listening to the water's beat.
Each reflection tells a child,
Stories held, both meek and wild.

Golden light through branches streams,
In this haven, we can dream.
Softly bend, the willows weave,
Patterns of the heart to leave.

Nature's magic softly sways,
In their arms, time gently stays.
Swaying willows, grace imbued,
In their presence, hearts subdued.

Embraces of Untamed Space

Under skies of endless blue,
Nature's breath invites us through.
Mountains rise and valleys fall,
In this vastness, we feel small.

Winds that carry whispers high,
In the open, hearts can fly.
Stars that twinkle like lost dreams,
In their light, hope softly beams.

Fields of gold and waves of green,
In this expanse, we are seen.
Embracing freedom's warm embrace,
Finding solace in this space.

Nature's canvas stretches wide,
A realm where wild souls abide.
In untamed space, we shall roam,
Every heartbeat finds its home.

The Hidden Dialogues of Earth

Beneath the soil, secrets weave,
Whispers of roots that gently cleave.
In every stone, a tale unfolds,
Of ancient dreams and futures bold.

Rivers murmur, lakes respond,
In quiet corners of the pond.
The winds carry songs from the past,
Echoes of wisdom, deep and fast.

Mountains stand, their silence loud,
Guardians of thoughts, beneath a shroud.
Listen closely, hear the call,
Nature speaks, inviting all.

In the twilight, shadows blend,
The cycle continues, without end.
In this dance of earth and sky,
The hidden dialogues never die.

Echoing Footprints in the Thicket

In the thicket where shadows lie,
Footprints whisper, soft and shy.
Each step taken, a tale appears,
Written in silence, held by years.

Branches murmur, leaves reply,
The secrets of the woods nearby.
Frogs croak softly, a rhythmic song,
In this haven, we all belong.

Moonlight glimmers on the ground,
Guiding late wanderers around.
Every echo, a memory's trace,
In this thicket, we find our place.

Time flows gently, a winding stream,
Trails of dreams, in twilight's gleam.
With every footstep, nature speaks,
In the thicket, the heart seeks.

Ballads of the Unfenced Horizon

Beyond the fences, freedom calls,
Where the sunset paints the walls.
Fields of gold and skies so wide,
In the distance, dreams abide.

Winds of change dance with the grain,
Whispers of joy, hints of pain.
Each horizon holds a story true,
Of paths once taken, and those anew.

Stars emerge in twilight's glow,
Guiding travelers, high and low.
In the silence, the heart can roam,
Finding solace, finding home.

Ballads echo in the night,
Songs of hope, of lost delight.
With every dawn, a chance to rise,
Chasing the dreams beyond the skies.

Shadows of the Enchanted Grove

In the grove where magic breathes,
Shadows dance among the leaves.
Underneath the ancient trees,
Stories linger in the breeze.

Moonbeams flirt with twilight's mist,
Each corner holds a hidden twist.
The nightingale sings a sweet refrain,
In this enchanted world, we remain.

Crickets chirp their tune of fate,
Binding spirits with threads of slate.
As lanterns flicker, stars align,
Guiding us through the sacred pine.

In the shadows, dreams ignite,
Illuminating the darkest night.
With every moment, the grove reveals,
The magic of what the heart feels.

Milton Keynes UK
Ingram Content Group UK Ltd.
UKHW020044271124
451585UK00012B/1045

9 789916 905432